Creating America

A History of the United States

McDougal Littell
A HOUGHTON MIFFLIN COMPANY

Printed in the United States of America

ISBN 0-618-15628-3
ISBN 0-618-16521-5

1 2 3 4 5 6 7 8 9 - RRW - 04 03 02 01

Contents

Guided Reading

A. Finding Main Ideas Fill out this chart with details about the two theories of how ancient people reached the Americas.

Theory One	Theory Two

B. Categorizing As you read about the development of Native American cultures, fill out the chart below by writing notes that describe the achievements of those cultures.

Culture	Achievements
1. The Olmec and Maya	
2. The Hohokam and Anasazi	
3. The Adena, Hopewell, and Mississippian	

Guided Reading

A. Categorizing As you read about early Native American cultures, take notes about the economy, technology, religious beliefs, and trading patterns of various groups.

1. Economy	2. Technology
3. Religious beliefs	**4. Trading patterns**

B. Finding Main Ideas On the back of this paper, note something significant you learned about each of the following Native American groups:

Inuit   Pomo   Aztec   Pueblo   Iroquois

Name _____   Date _____

Guided Reading

A. Analyzing Causes and Recognizing Effects As you read about the empires and states that arose in West Africa, briefly note the causes or effects (depending on which is missing) of each situation.

Causes	Effects
1.	By 1500, Africa had been linked to the rest of the world for centuries.
2. The king of Ghana taxed all the gold and salt passing through his kingdom.	
3.	A Muslim army conquered Kumbi Saleh, weakening Ghana's power.
4. Mali was located farther south than Ghana.	
5. The legend of Mali's wealth spread to Europe.	
6.	Moroccan troops quickly defeated the Songhai warriors.
7. Benin was located on main trade routes.	

B. Finding Main Ideas On the back of this paper, briefly identify each term or name.

Ghana   Islam   Mali   Songhai   Yoruba

Guided Reading

A. Recognizing Effects As you read this section, fill out the chart below by writing answers in the appropriate boxes.

	How did Europeans respond?
1. Viking raids	
2. Increased stability caused by feudalism	
3. Muslim control of Holy Land	
4. Weakening of feudalism and suffering caused by plague	
5. Italian wealth from Asian trade	

B. Finding Main Ideas On the back of this paper, define or explain each of the following:

feudalism   manor system   Renaissance   printing press   Reformation

Name _____ Date _____

Guided Reading

A. Sequencing Events As you read about the age of exploration, take notes to
answer questions about events listed in the time line.

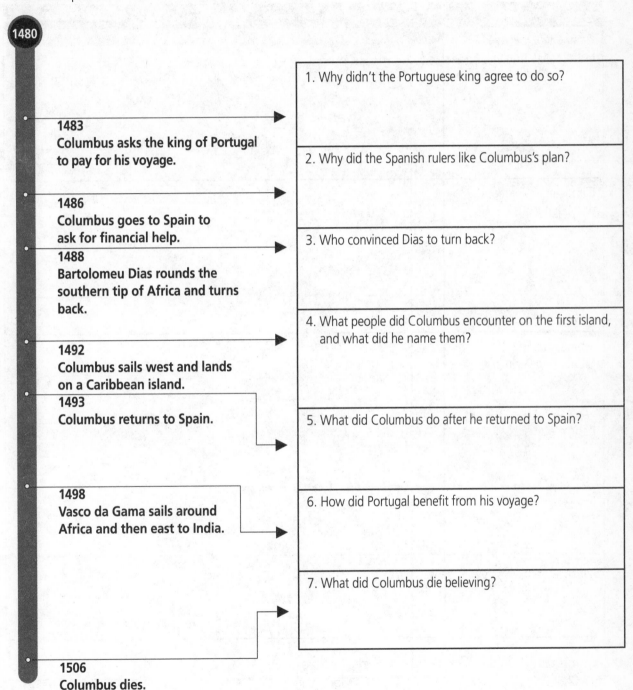

1480

1483
Columbus asks the king of Portugal
to pay for his voyage.

1486
Columbus goes to Spain to
ask for financial help.

1488
Bartolomeu Dias rounds the
southern tip of Africa and turns
back.

1492
Columbus sails west and lands
on a Caribbean island.

1493
Columbus returns to Spain.

1498
Vasco da Gama sails around
Africa and then east to India.

1506
Columbus dies.

1. Why didn't the Portuguese king agree to do so?

2. Why did the Spanish rulers like Columbus's plan?

3. Who convinced Dias to turn back?

4. What people did Columbus encounter on the first island,
and what did he name them?

5. What did Columbus do after he returned to Spain?

6. How did Portugal benefit from his voyage?

7. What did Columbus die believing?

B. Analyzing Causes On the back of this paper, explain the mistakes that Columbus
made in his plans for his journey to Asia.

Chapter **2** *Section 1 Spain Claims an Empire*

Guided Reading

A. Taking Notes As you read this section, take notes on the following topics.

	Notes
Competition between Spain and Portugal	
European exploration of foreign lands	
Spain's invasions of Mexico and Peru	
Reasons for Spain's success	

B. Summarizing On the back of this paper, identify or explain each of the following:

mercantilism   Hernando Cortés   Montezuma

Name _____ Date _____

Guided Reading

A. Finding Main Ideas As you read this section, answer the questions next to the time line.

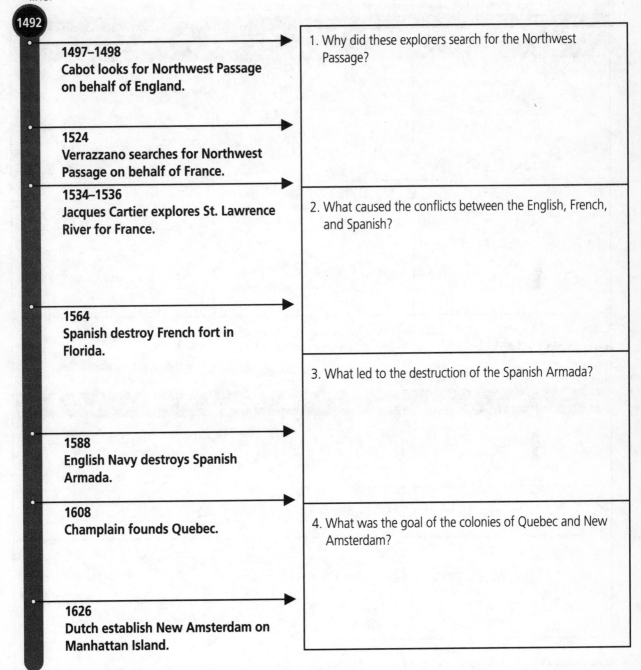

1492

1497–1498
Cabot looks for Northwest Passage on behalf of England.

1524
Verrazzano searches for Northwest Passage on behalf of France.

1534–1536
Jacques Cartier explores St. Lawrence River for France.

1564
Spanish destroy French fort in Florida.

1588
English Navy destroys Spanish Armada.

1608
Champlain founds Quebec.

1626
Dutch establish New Amsterdam on Manhattan Island.

1. Why did these explorers search for the Northwest Passage?

2. What caused the conflicts between the English, French, and Spanish?

3. What led to the destruction of the Spanish Armada?

4. What was the goal of the colonies of Quebec and New Amsterdam?

B. Summarizing On the back of this paper, identify or define each of the following:

Spanish Armada   New France

EUROPEAN EXPLORATION OF THE AMERICAS **7**

Guided Reading

A. Categorizing As you read, use the chart below to categorize the information in the section on the Spanish colonies in the Americas.

Colonial Government	Relations with Native Americans	Colonial Economy

B. Recognizing Effects Use the chart below to take notes on the effects of the Columbian Exchange.

	Effects of the Columbian Exchange
Effects on the Americas	
Effects on Europe	

Name _____ Date _____

Guided Reading

A. Finding Main Ideas As you read this section, fill out the chart below on the beginnings of slavery in the Americas.

Issue	Notes
1. Origins of Slave Labor	Main Idea: Details:
2. The Slave Trade and Middle Passage	Main Idea: Details:
3. Slave Codes and Racism	Main Idea: Details:

B. Summarizing On the back of this paper, identify or explain each of the following:

African Diaspora   middle passage   racism

Name _____   Date _____

Guided Reading

A. Finding Main Ideas As you read about Roanoke, Sagadahoc, and Jamestown, use the following questions to help you summarize ideas in this section.

1. **Who?** Who were among the settlers at Sagadahoc? Who was their leader?	
2. **What?** What happened to the colonists at Roanoke? What happened to the colony at Sagadahoc?	
3. **When?** When was Jamestown settled? When did the "starving time" end?	
4. **Why?** Why did the settlers go to Jamestown? Why didn't the settlers get along with their neighbors? Why did Jamestown nearly fail?	
5. **Where?** Where was Roanoke? Where was Sagadahoc? Where was Jamestown?	
6. **How?** How was Jamestown saved from failure?	

B. Summarizing On the back of this paper, explain the importance for the Virginia Colony of each of the following:

House of Burgesses   indentured servant   Bacon's Rebellion

Guided Reading

A. Analyzing Causes and Recognizing Effects As you read this section, fill out the chart below by writing notes that summarize the causes and results of the conflicts.

	Causes of the Conflict	Results of the Conflict
1. Puritans *vs.* the Church of England		
2. Puritan leaders *vs.* Roger Williams		
3. Puritan leaders *vs.* Anne Hutchinson		
4. King Philip's War		
5. Salem witchcraft trials		

B. Categorizing On the back of this paper, create a word web for each of the following:

Pilgrims   Great Migration   Mayflower Compact

Guided Reading

Summarizing As you read about the New England and Southern colonies, fill out the chart below by writing notes that describe aspects of each colony.

Middle Colonies			
1. New York—Population	2. Pennsylvania—Religion	3. Pennsylvania—Relations with Native Americans	4. New Jersey—Proprietor

Southern Colonies			
5. Georgia—Relations with England	6. The Carolinas—Population	7. Maryland—Religion	8. The Carolinas—Relations with Native Americans

Name _____ Date _____

Guided Reading

A. Finding Main Ideas As you read about the development of the New England Colonies, fill in the diagram below with notes about what made the region unique.

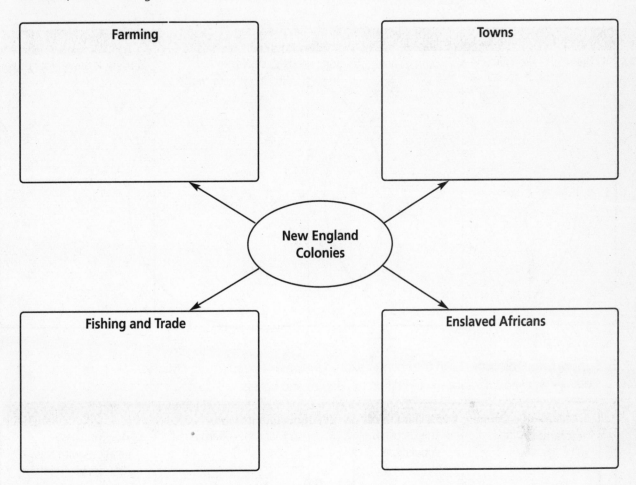

Farming

Towns

New England Colonies

Fishing and Trade

Enslaved Africans

B. Analyzing Causes The Puritan religion gradually declined in New England during the 1700s. Use the chart below to take notes about the causes of the decline.

1.

2.

3.

Decline of the Puritan Religion

Guided Reading

A. Comparing and Contrasting As you read this section, compare and contrast the Middle Colonies with the New England Colonies.

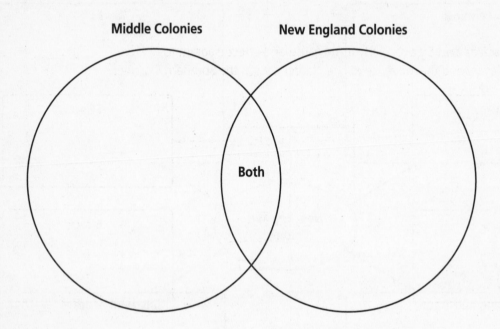

Middle Colonies   **New England Colonies**

Both

B. Supporting Opinions Fill in the chart to explain why many people in the Middle Colonies showed tolerance toward different peoples and beliefs.

1. The Middle Colonies had a climate of tolerance.	2. Supporting Reasons a. b.

C. Recognizing Effects How did the large cash crops that were grown in the Middle Colonies affect the development of the region's cities?

Guided Reading

A. Drawing Conclusions What effect did the self-sufficiency of Southern plantations have on the growth of cities in the South?

B. Recognizing Causes and Effects Fill out the cause-and-effect diagram to analyze the growth of slavery and the influence of the planter class in the Southern Colonies.

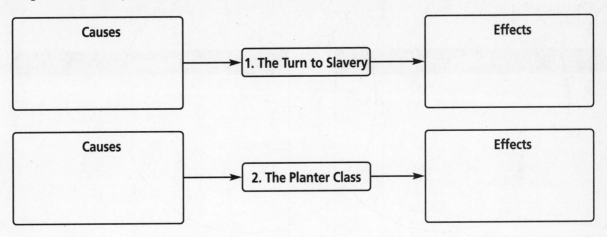

Causes		Effects
	1. The Turn to Slavery	
Causes		Effects
	2. The Planter Class	

C. Summarizing Use the chart to give examples of how enslaved Africans maintained many traditional customs and resisted slavery.

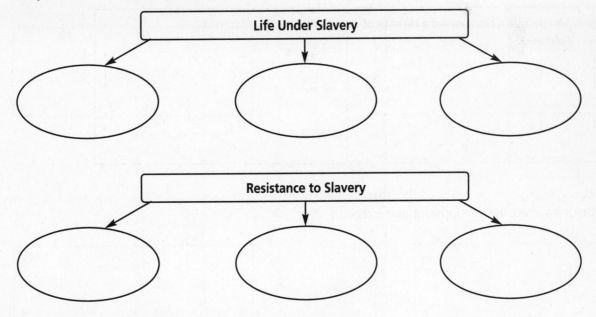

Life Under Slavery

Resistance to Slavery

Guided Reading

A. Summarizing What were some of the important features of the Backcountry's geography?

B. Categorizing In the boxes below, briefly describe the lives of the first Backcountry settlers.

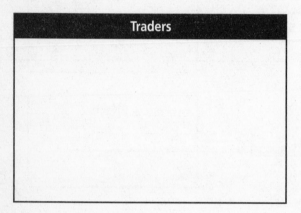

Traders

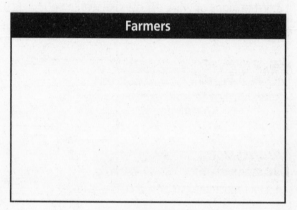

Farmers

C. Finding Main Ideas Use the chart below to list some of the different groups that inhabited North America. Also, briefly describe which areas the different groups lived in or claimed.

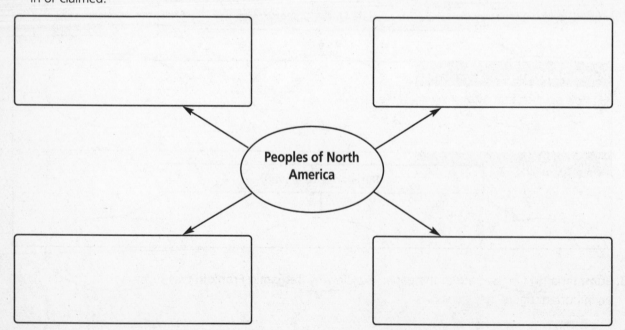

Peoples of North America

Guided Reading

A. Finding Main Ideas As you read this section, take notes to answer questions about parts of colonial culture.

| **Land** |
| 1. Why was owning land important to colonists? |

| **Women** |
| 2. What kinds of work did colonial women do? |

| **Young People** |
| 3. What kinds of work did young people do? |

| **Education** |
| 4. How much education did colonists have? |

| **Publishing** |
| 5. What was published in the colonies? |

| **Great Awakening** |
| 6. How did the Great Awakening affect the colonies? |

| **Enlightenment** |
| 7. What Enlightenment ideas influenced colonists? |

B. Summarizing On the back of this paper, explain why **Benjamin Franklin** was such an important figure in the colonies.

Guided Reading

A. Categorizing As you read, note whether each term is linked to a gain (+) or loss (–) of rights for English citizens or colonists. In the last column, name the rights connected with the term.

Term	Rights gained (+) or lost (–)?	Which rights?
1. Magna Carta		
2. Parliament		
3. Colonial assemblies		
4. Edmund Andros		
5. English Bill of Rights		
6. salutary neglect		
7. Zenger trial		

B. Contrasting On the back of this paper, make a chart contrasting the powers of the royal governor and the colonial assembly in governing the colonies.

Guided Reading

A. Finding Main Ideas Fill out the chart below as you read about the French and
Indian War (1754–1763).

1. Which groups fought against each other?	2. Why did they fight?	3. Where were important battles in the war?
4. Who were military officers or political leaders involved in the war?	5. How did the war end?	6. What happened after the war?

B. Analyzing Points of View The Treaty of Paris (1763) divided North America among
European powers. On the back of this paper, explain how England, France, and Spain
probably viewed the terms of the treaty.

Guided Reading

A. Solving Problems As you read this section, fill in the second column of the chart below with more details about the British attempts to solve their problems. In the third column, explain how the colonists responded to each of those solutions.

Britain's Problems	Britain's Solutions	Colonists' Responses
1. Preventing Native American uprisings	Proclamation Act (1763):	
2. Keeping peace in the American colonies	Quartering Act (1765):	
3. Paying for war debts	Sugar Act (1764):	
	Stamp Act (1765):	
4. Maintaining power over the American colonies	Declaratory Act (1766):	

B. Summarizing On the back of this paper, briefly explain the importance of each of the following in protesting British policies.

Patrick Henry   boycott   Sons of Liberty

Chapter **6** *Section 2 Colonial Resistance Grows*

Guided Reading

A. Finding Main Ideas As you read pages 164–165 of this section, fill in the cluster diagrams with historical events, examples, or people that relate to the main idea questions below.

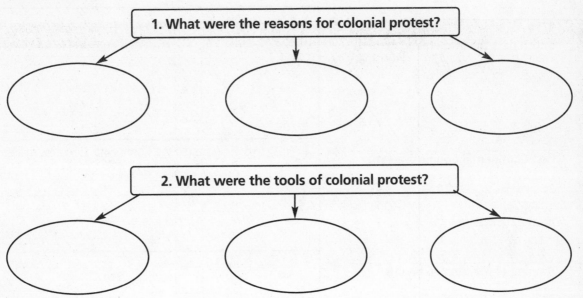

1. What were the reasons for colonial protest?

2. What were the tools of colonial protest?

B. Analyzing Causes and Recognizing Effects Fill out the cause-and-effect diagram to analyze the following British actions.

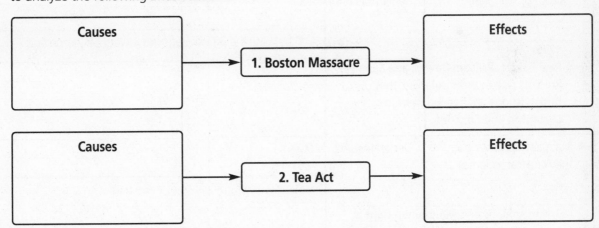

| Causes | 1. Boston Massacre | Effects |

| Causes | 2. Tea Act | Effects |

C. Forming and Supporting Opinions Fill in the chart to explain why you either approve or disapprove of the Boston Tea Party as a method of protest.

1. Your Opinion of the Boston Tea Party	2. Supporting Reasons a. b. c.

Name _____   Date _____

Guided Reading

A. Sequencing Events As you read this section, answer the questions about events shown in the time line below.

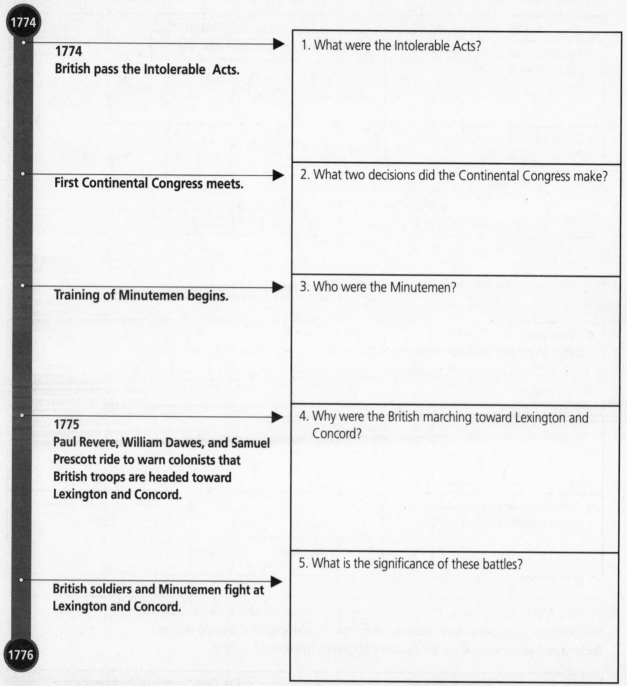

1774

1774
British pass the Intolerable Acts.

1. What were the Intolerable Acts?

First Continental Congress meets.

2. What two decisions did the Continental Congress make?

Training of Minutemen begins.

3. Who were the Minutemen?

1775
Paul Revere, William Dawes, and Samuel Prescott ride to warn colonists that British troops are headed toward Lexington and Concord.

4. Why were the British marching toward Lexington and Concord?

5. What is the significance of these battles?

British soldiers and Minutemen fight at Lexington and Concord.

1776

B. Analyzing Points of View On the back of this paper, briefly explain the sides that Patriots and Loyalists took during the Revolutionary War.

Chapter **6** Section 4 Declaring Independence

Guided Reading

A. Categorizing As you read this section, fill in the chart below with information about Americans' political and military actions at the outbreak of the Revolutionary War.

Political Actions	Outcomes
1. Second Continental Congress meets (May 1775).	
2. Congress drafts the Olive Branch Petition (July 1775).	

Military Actions	Outcomes
3. Americans attack Fort Ticonderoga (May 1775).	
4. Continental Army fights in the Battle of Bunker Hill (June 1775).	
5. Continental Army invades Quebec (November 1775).	
6. Continental Army surrounds British forces in Boston (January 1776).	

B. Finding Main Ideas In the boxes below, write two newspaper headlines that tell the important ideas about each document shown. Your headline should address these questions: Who wrote the document? What is it about?

Common Sense		The Declaration of Independence
1.		2.

Name _____ Date _____

Guided Reading

A. Finding Main Ideas As you read the Declaration of Independence, fill in the diagram below with key points about the main parts of the document.

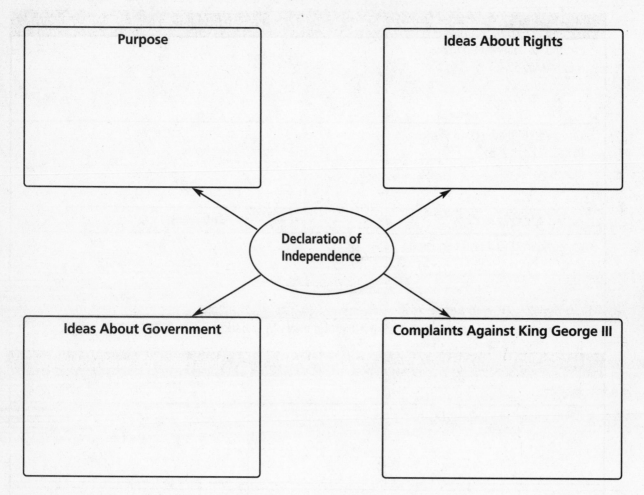

| Purpose | Ideas About Rights |

Declaration of Independence

| Ideas About Government | Complaints Against King George III |

B. Evaluating Review the complaints against King George III that you listed in the box above. Using a number scale, rate the complaints from most important to least important. Record your numbers in the box.

C. Forming and Supporting Opinions Which part of the Declaration do you think is the most meaningful for today? Explain why on the back of this paper.

Guided Reading

A. Categorizing Use the chart below to take notes about who chose the Patriot side and who chose the Loyalist side.

Patriots	Loyalists

B. Analyzing Causes and Recognizing Effects As you read this section, write answers to the questions about each of the Revolutionary War battles listed below.

	Who won?	Why did they win?	What were the important results?
1. New York			
2. Trenton			
3. Saratoga			

Chapter **7** *Section 2 The War Expands*

Guided Reading

A. Categorizing As you read this section, take notes about people who helped to win American independence.

1. Marquis de Lafayette	2. Baron von Steuben
3. George Rogers Clark	4. John Paul Jones

B. Finding Main Ideas On the back of this paper, explain or define each of the following terms:

ally   privateer

Guided Reading

A. Analyzing Causes and Recognizing Effects As you read this section, write answers to the questions about each of the Revolutionary War battles listed below.

	Who won?	Why did they win?	What were the important results?
1. Charles Town			
2. Camden			
3. Yorktown			

B. Summarizing What were the difficulties faced by each group of Patriots during the Revolutionary War?

Patriots	What were some of the hardships they faced?
Civilians	
Soldiers	
Guerrilla Fighters	

C. Finding Main Ideas On the back of this paper, identify or define each of the following terms.

Lord Cornwallis   pacifist

Name _____ Date _____

Chapter **7** *Section 4 The Legacy of the War*

Guided Reading

A. Analyzing Causes As you read this section, use the chart below to take notes about the advantages that led to America's victory.

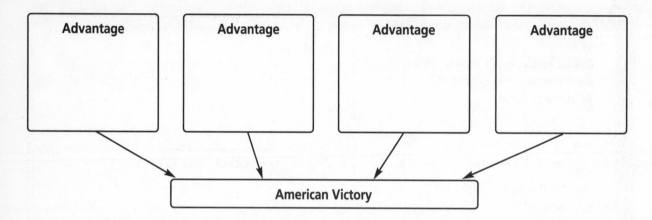

| Advantage | Advantage | Advantage | Advantage |

American Victory

B. Recognizing Effects Use the chart below to take notes about the legacy of the war.

Terms of the Treaty	Costs of the War	Issues After the War

Chapter **8** *Section 1 The Confederation Era*

Guided Reading

Sequencing Events As you read this section, answer the questions about the events shown on the time line below.

1775

1775
Daniel Boone leads settlers into Kentucky and helps build the Wilderness Road.

1. What did the American settlers find when they reached Kentucky?

1781
The Articles of Confederation take effect.

2. Why did the Articles of Confederation not take effect until 1781?

1785
Congress passes the Land Ordinance of 1785.

3. What did the Land Ordinance of 1785 do?

1787
Daniel Shays leads a rebellion of farmers against the state legislature in Massachusetts.

4. Why did Masssachusetts farmers rebel against their state legislature?

1787
Congress passes the Northwest Ordinance.

5. How was the Northwest Ordinance different than the Land Ordinance of 1785?

Name _____ Date _____

Guided Reading

A. Making Generalizations As you read the section, take notes on the characteristics of the people who served as delegates to the Convention.

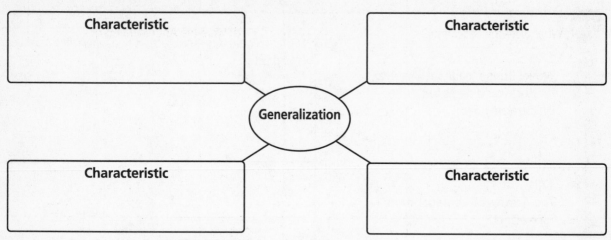

B. Summarizing Use the chart below to summarize the Virginia Plan and the New Jersey Plan.

1. The Virginia Plan proposed a legislature that consisted of:	2. The New Jersey Plan proposed a legislature that consisted of:
3. Who supported the Virginia Plan?	4. Who supported the New Jersey Plan?
5. How did the Great Compromise settle this issue?	

C. Analyzing Points of View On the back of this paper, briefly explain the disagreement between Northerners and Southerners that was settled by the Three-Fifths Compromise.

Chapter **8** *Section 3 Ratifying the Constitution*

Guided Reading

A. Analyzing Points of View As you read the section, take notes on the people and ideas involved in the debate over ratification of the Constitution.

1. What were the Federalists?	2. What were the Antifederalists?
3. Who were the leading Federalists?	4. Who were the leading Antifederalists?
5. What reasons did the Federalists give to defend their views on the ratification?	6. What reasons did the Antifederalists give to defend their views on the Constitution?

B. Summarizing On the back of this paper, summarize the arguments in favor of adding a bill of rights to the Constitution.

Name _____   Date _____

Guided Reading

A. Finding Main Ideas As you read the Preamble, fill in the cluster diagram with the six goals of the Constitution.

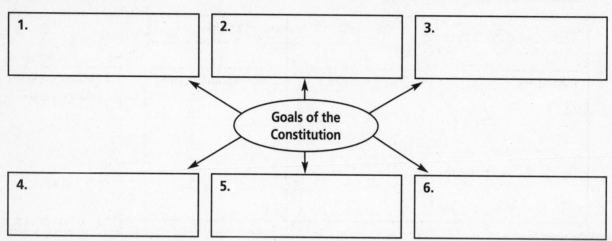

B. Comparing and Contrasting As you read about Congress in Article 1, fill in the chart with information about the House of Representatives and the Senate.

	House of Representatives	Senate
1. Candidates' requirements		
2. Term of office		
3. Number of members per state		
4. Impeachment		
5. Bills for raising money		
6. Military powers		
7. Role of vice president		

Guided Reading

A. Summarizing As you read Article 2, fill in the diagram with examples of the president's powers and duties.

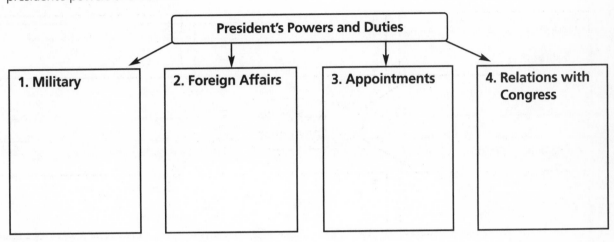

President's Powers and Duties

1. Military	2. Foreign Affairs	3. Appointments	4. Relations with Congress

B. Finding Main Ideas As you read Article 3, fill out the chart below with important information about the judicial branch of government.

1. What courts make up the judicial branch of government?

2. What is the term of office for a Supreme Court judge?

3. What is judicial power? Give two examples.

4. What "check," or control, does the Supreme Court have on Congress? Explain.

5. How does the Constitution define *treason*? What must happen before a person is convicted of treason?

Guided Reading

A. Solving Problems As you read Article 4, explain how the Constitution solves each problem listed below.

> **1. Problem:** A major U.S. city is the scene of domestic violence, and many people in the state are in danger.
>
> **Solution:**

> **2. Problem:** A person is charged with a serious crime in one state and then flees to another state.
>
> **Solution:**

B. Summarizing As you read Article 5, explain the procedures for amending the Constitution.

1. Proposing Amendments	2. Ratifying Amendments

C. Summarizing As you read Article 6, complete the diagram below to show the bases for the "supreme law of the land."

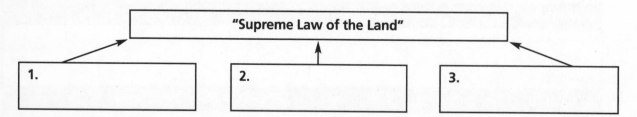

"Supreme Law of the Land"

1.

2.

3.

D. Finding Main Ideas As you read Article 7, answer the following questions.

1. How many states had to ratify the Constitution before it could go into effect?

    _____

2. In what year was the Constitution signed by the delegates to the Constitutional Convention? _____

Guided Reading

Categorizing As you read Amendments 1–27, fill in the chart below with a brief explanation of each amendment. Use the groupings shown as a guide.

Explanation

Personal Freedom Amendment 1 Amendment 2 Amendment 3 Amendment 4	
Fair Legal Treatment Amendment 5 Amendment 6 Amendment 7 Amendment 8	
Reserved Powers Amendment 9 Amendment 10	
Election Procedures and Conditions of Office Amendment 12 Amendment 17 Amendment 20 Amendment 22 Amendment 25 Amendment 27	
Social and Economic Changes Amendment 11 Amendment 13 Amendment 14 Amendment 16 Amendment 18 Amendment 21	
Voting Rights Amendment 15 Amendment 19 Amendment 23 Amendment 24 Amendment 26	

Guided Reading

A. Taking Notes Fill out the chart below, taking notes about Washington's presidency.

The Courts
1. What did the Judiciary Act of 1789 establish?

↓

The Cabinet
2. What departments did Washington create, and whom did he appoint to head them?

↓

Economic Policy
3. Why did Jefferson and Madison oppose the national bank?   4. Why did Hamilton support the national bank?

↓

Interpreting the Constitution
5. What are loose and strict constructions of the Constitution, and who favored each?

B. Summarizing On the back of this paper, briefly define each of the following.

cabinet   tariff   Federal Judiciary Act

Name _____   Date _____

Guided Reading

A. Finding Main Ideas As you read about the U.S. government's first experiences with challenges to its authority, take notes to answer questions about events appearing on the time line.

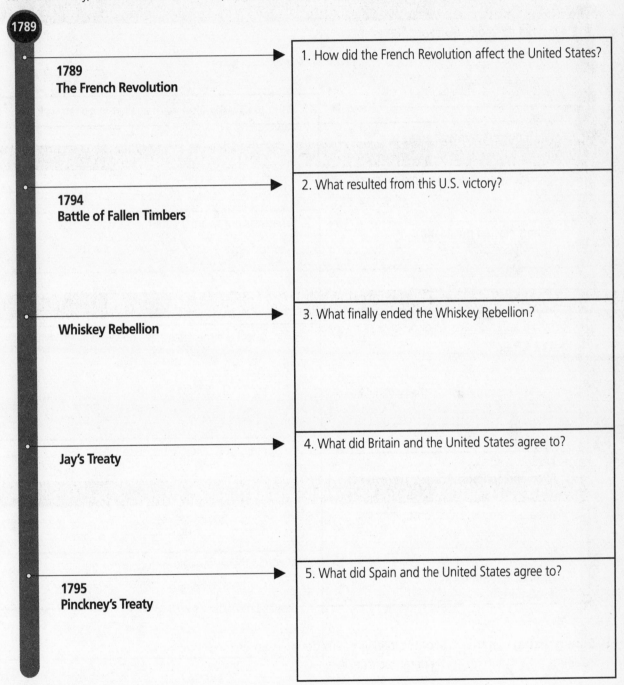

1789

1789
The French Revolution

1. How did the French Revolution affect the United States?

1794
Battle of Fallen Timbers

2. What resulted from this U.S. victory?

Whiskey Rebellion

3. What finally ended the Whiskey Rebellion?

Jay's Treaty

4. What did Britain and the United States agree to?

1795
Pinckney's Treaty

5. What did Spain and the United States agree to?

B. Summarizing On the back of this paper, identify or explain each of the following.

Little Turtle   John Jay   Treaty of Greenville

Guided Reading

A. Finding Main Ideas As you read about the growth of political parties and the presidency of John Adams, take notes to answer questions about events appearing on the time line.

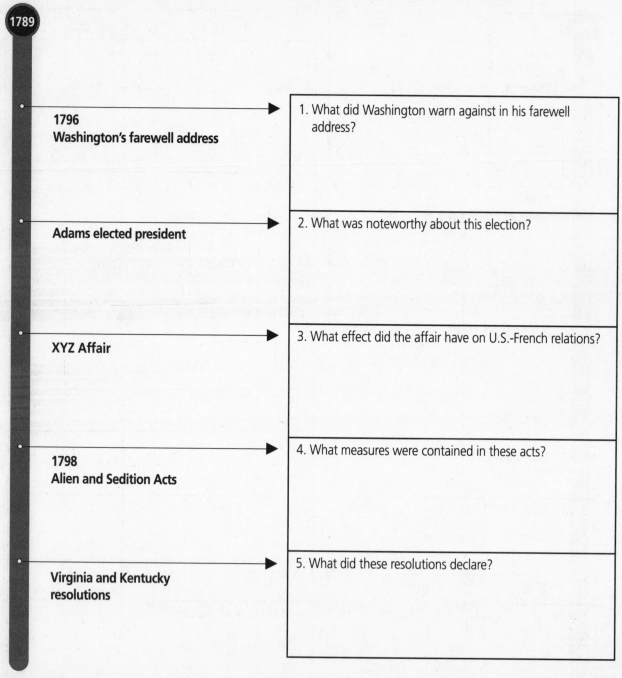

1789

1796
Washington's farewell address

1. What did Washington warn against in his farewell address?

Adams elected president

2. What was noteworthy about this election?

XYZ Affair

3. What effect did the affair have on U.S.-French relations?

1798
Alien and Sedition Acts

4. What measures were contained in these acts?

Virginia and Kentucky resolutions

5. What did these resolutions declare?

B. Summarizing On the back of this paper, identify or explain each of the following.

XYZ Affair   Alien and Sedition Acts   states' rights

Name _____ Date _____

Guided Reading

A. Sequencing Events As you read about the presidential election of 1800, fill in the boxes below with descriptions of the events leading up to the election of Thomas Jefferson.

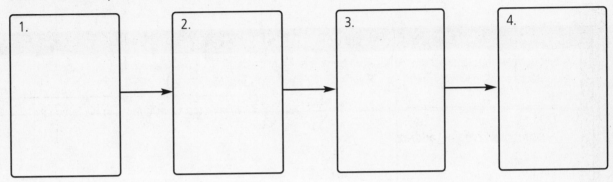

1. ___

2. ___

3. ___

4. ___

B. Summarizing As you read about the early years of Thomas Jefferson's presidency, answer the questions below.

Thomas Jefferson Takes Office
1. What were Jefferson's views on the kind of country the United States ought to be?
2. How did Jefferson simplify the federal government?
3. Why did Jefferson have little power over the judiciary?
4. What were the results of the Supreme Court's decision in *Marbury* v. *Madison?*

C. Comparing On the back of this paper, explain how each of the following are related.

Judiciary Act of 1801   John Marshall   judicial review

Guided Reading

A. Comparing and Contrasting As you read about the West in 1800, compare and contrast the activity taking place in the different regions west of the Appalachian Mountains.

The West in 1800		
1. Area between the Appalachian Mountains and the Mississippi River	2. Area between the Mississippi River and the Rocky Mountains	3. Area along the Pacific Coast
Similarities:		

B. Analyzing Causes As you read about the Louisiana Purchase, write down the reasons that Napoleon might have had for selling the Louisiana Territory to the United States.

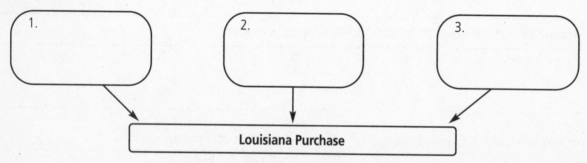

1.

2.

3.

Louisiana Purchase

C. Recognizing Effects What were the most important results of the expeditions into the Louisiana Territory in the early 1800s?

Chapter **10** *Section 3 Problems with Foreign Powers*

Guided Reading

A. Solving Problems Take notes describing how President Jefferson and Chief Tecumseh responded to the problems described below. Then explain why their responses succeeded, failed, or had mixed results in solving the problem.

1. President Thomas Jefferson	
Problem: War in Europe resulted in the seizure of U.S. ships by both France and Britain. It also resulted in the impressment of Americans into the British navy.	**Response:**
Reasons for the success or failure of Jefferson's response:	

2. Shawnee Chief Tecumseh	
Problem: As white settlers moved into the Ohio valley by the thousands, Native Americans continued to lose their land.	**Response:**
Reasons for the success or failure of Tecumseh's response:	

B. Forming and Supporting Opinions Fill in the chart to explain why you approve or disapprove of the U.S. declaration of war against Great Britain in 1812.

1. Your opinion of the U.S. declaration of war in June 1812:	2. Supporting Reasons a. b. c.

Guided Reading

A. Sequencing Events As you read this section, take notes about the different phases of the war, and record the major events of each phase.

The War of 1812
First Phase (1812–1814)
1.
2.
3.
4.
5.
Second Phase (1814–1815)
1.
2.
3.
4.
5.

B. Recognizing Effects As you read about the War of 1812, take notes on the legacy of the war in the United States.

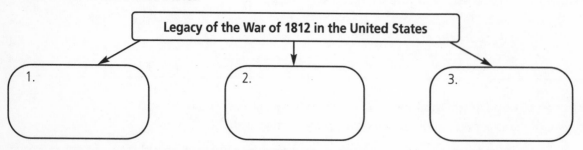

Legacy of the War of 1812 in the United States

1.

2.

3.

C. Summarizing On the back of this paper, briefly explain the relationship between each of the following.

Fort McHenry   Francis Scott Key   Star-Spangled Banner

Guided Reading

A. Recognizing Effects Fill in the chart as you read this section, noting how each development of the early 1800s affected the nation.

Development	Effects
1. Textile mills	
2. Interchangeable parts	
3. New inventions • steamboat • telegraph • steel plow • mechanical reaper • threshing machine	

B. Categorizing On the back of this paper, write what each person built or promoted that helped the nation grow.

Samuel Slater   Eli Whitney   Samuel F. B. Morse

Francis Cabot Lowell   Robert Fulton   John Deere

Name _____   Date _____

Guided Reading

A. Recognizing Effects As you read pages 348–350, fill in the cluster diagram with effects of the cotton gin.

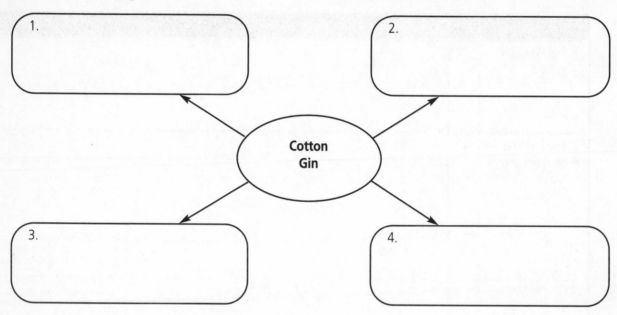

1.

2.

Cotton Gin

3.

4.

B. Categorizing As you read pages 350–353, fill in the chart with details about each category of Southerners.

Slaveholding whites	Nonslaveholding whites	Enslaved blacks	Free blacks

C. Drawing Conclusions On the back of this paper, briefly describe Nat Turner's rebellion and its results. Then draw one conclusion about Southern slavery, based on what you learned about the rebellion.

Guided Reading

A. Finding Main Ideas Fill in the chart as you read pages 354–357. Note how each force moved the United States toward growth or national unity.

Force	How It Led to Growth or National Unity
1. The American System	
2. The building of roads and canals	
3. Supreme Court decisions	
4. Boundary settlements	

B. Analyzing Points of View Fill in the diagram as you read about admitting Missouri to statehood, on pages 357–359. Explain what the North wanted, what the South wanted, and what the Missouri Compromise offered both sides.

North:	South:

Missouri Compromise:

C. Summarizing On the back of this paper, summarize the message of the Monroe Doctrine and the events that led President Monroe to issue it.

Guided Reading

A. Summarizing As you read this section on the politics of the 1820s, summarize the information in the chart below.

1. Who were the candidates in the 1824 presidential election and their supporters?	2. What was the outcome of the 1824 election?
3. What happened as a result of the 1824 election?	4. How did expanding democracy bring Andrew Jackson to power?
5. What qualities made Andrew Jackson a popular candidate and leader?	6. What were the characteristics of Jacksonian democracy?

B. Drawing Conclusions What changes in the United States did Jackson's election signal?

Name _____ Date _____

Guided Reading

A. Sequencing Events As you read this section, answer the questions about events shown in the time line below.

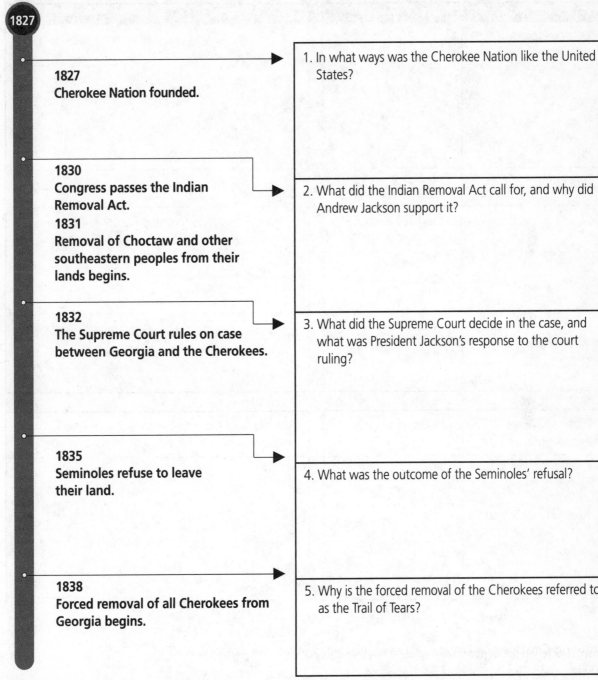

1827
Cherokee Nation founded.

1. In what ways was the Cherokee Nation like the United States?

1830
Congress passes the Indian Removal Act.
1831
Removal of Choctaw and other southeastern peoples from their lands begins.

2. What did the Indian Removal Act call for, and why did Andrew Jackson support it?

1832
The Supreme Court rules on case between Georgia and the Cherokees.

3. What did the Supreme Court decide in the case, and what was President Jackson's response to the court ruling?

1835
Seminoles refuse to leave their land.

4. What was the outcome of the Seminoles' refusal?

1838
Forced removal of all Cherokees from Georgia begins.

5. Why is the forced removal of the Cherokees referred to as the Trail of Tears?

B. Summarizing On the back of this paper, briefly explain the importance of the following in the conflict over the removal of Native Americans from their lands.

Indian Removal Act   Indian Territory   Black Hawk War

Chapter **12** *Section 3 Conflicts Over States' Rights*

Guided Reading

A. Taking Notes As you read this section, take notes on the following topics related to the conflict over states' rights.

States' Rights Conflict	Notes
1. Key players	
2. Key events	
3. Causes	
4. Results	

B. Comparing and Contrasting On the back of this paper, briefly compare and contrast the views of Thomas Jefferson and John C. Calhoun on the doctrine of nullification.

Guided Reading

A. Recognizing Effects As you read this section, briefly note the effects of each event or situation.

Event/Situation	Effects
1. Nicholas Biddle asks Congress to renew the charter of the Second Bank of the United States in 1832.	
2. veto of charter renewal and deposit of federal funds in state banks	
3. State banks use federal deposits to issue large amounts of paper money.	
4. widespread fear about the economy	
5. Banks go out of business.	
6. Economic slump causes hardships and affects politics.	

B. Recognizing Propaganda On the back of this page, briefly explain how the Whig Party used propaganda to promote William Henry Harrison, its candidate in the 1840 election.

Name _____   Date _____

Guided Reading

A. Categorizing As you read about expansion to areas of the West, fill out the chart.

	New Mexico	Oregon	Utah
1. Who went?			
2. Why did they go?			
3. How did they get there?			
4. What did they find when they got there?			

B. Taking Notes Identify each person or group and explain an important contribution of that person or group.

Mountain men	**Marcus and Narcissa Whitman**
Land speculators	**The Sager family**
Mormons	**William Becknell**

Chapter 13 Section 2 The Texas Revolution

Guided Reading

A. Sequencing Events As you read this section, answer questions about the time line.

1821

Spain offers land grants to anyone bringing settlers to Texas. Mexico gains its independence from Spain.

1. Why did Spain want people to settle in Texas? What effect did Mexico's independence have on Stephen Austin's land grant?

2. Why did Americans want to settle in Texas?

1823

1824

3. What brought American settlers into conflict with the Mexican government?

1835

The Texas Revolution is led by Texans eager to gain independence from Mexico.

4. What happened at the Alamo?

1836

The Republic of Texas is founded and asks the U.S. government to annex the new republic.

5. Why was the United States reluctant to annex Texas?

B. Evaluating What role did *Tejanos* and Texans play in the Texas Revolution? Explain.

Guided Reading

A. Summarizing As you read this section, fill in the blanks in the following summary.

The United States angered Mexico when the U.S. government annexed Texas and

admitted it as a state in 1845. In addition, Mexico and the United States disagreed

about the location of Texas's (1) _____. U.S. President

(2) _____ sent John Slidell to Mexico with an offer to buy the disputed

land in Texas and the Mexican-owned territories of (3) _____ and

(4) _____. Mexico declined the offer.

When (5) _____'s troops blockaded the (6) _____,

Mexico saw the action as an invasion and ambushed an American patrol. In response,

President Polk successfully got Congress to declare war. Next, General Stephen

Kearny captured (7) _____ without bloodshed. In the meantime, American

settlers in (8) _____, led by John C. Frémont, overthrew the Mexican

government there and established an independent nation called the

(9) _____. Later that year U.S. troops arrived, and Americans soon

controlled all of California.

In September 1846, General (10) _____'s troops moved south from

(11) _____ into northern Mexico and captured the city of Monterrey. In

February 1847, (12) _____'s Mexican troops and Zachary Taylor's U.S.

forces met at the Battle of (13) _____. The Mexicans lost. Meanwhile,

General Winfield Scott moved toward (14) _____ and captured the capital.

The Treaty of (15) _____ ended the war, and it forced Mexico

to cede nearly one-half of its territory to the United States. The United States added

more land in 1853 with the (16) _____, which stretched across what is

now southern New Mexico and Arizona.

B. Comparing and Contrasting What was Antonio López de Santa Anna's role in
both the Texas Revolution and the War with Mexico?

Chapter **13** Section 4 The California Gold Rush

Guided Reading

A. Analyzing Causes and Recognizing Effects As you read this section, fill in the chart below.

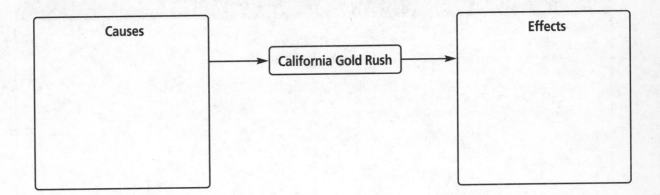

| Causes | | Effects |

B. Forming and Supporting Opinions What do you think was the most significant effect of the gold rush?

Most significant effect:	Supporting reasons:
	a.
	b.
	c.

C. Drawing Conclusions How did the California gold rush create major problems between Northern free states and Southern slave states?

Name _____ Date _____

Guided Reading

A. Analyzing Causes As you read this section, use the chart below to take notes about the reasons why people migrated to the United States.

Push Factors	Pull Factors

B. Finding Main Ideas Use the chart below to take notes about where different immigrant groups settled in the United States and why.

	Where did they settle?	Why did they settle there?
Scandinavians		
Germans		
Irish		

C. Recognizing Effects On the back of this page, explain how some Americans responded to the immigrants.

Guided Reading

A. Finding Main Ideas As you read this section, use the chart below to take notes about how writers and artists of the 1800s created truly American works.

American Writers	American Artists

B. Categorizing Use the chart below to list important details about each writer's work.

Writer	Important details about work
Ralph Waldo Emerson	
Henry David Thoreau	
Walt Whitman	
Emily Dickinson	
Edgar Allan Poe	
Nathaniel Hawthorne	
Herman Melville	

Guided Reading

A. Recognizing Effects As you read this section, use the chart below to record what was taught at revivals and why that led to a reform movement.

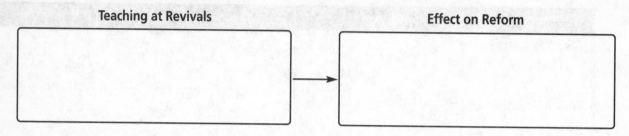

Teaching at Revivals   **Effect on Reform**

B. Categorizing Use the chart below to list important details about each reform movement of the mid-1800s.

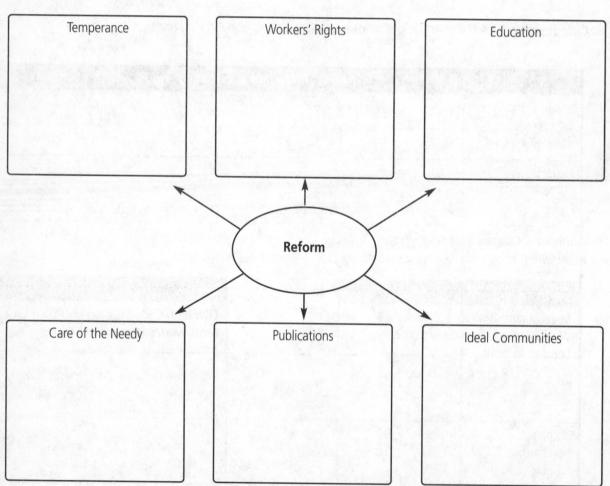

Temperance   Workers' Rights   Education

Reform

Care of the Needy   Publications   Ideal Communities

Guided Reading

A. Solving Problems As you read this section, use the chart below to record what actions the following people took to oppose slavery.

People	Actions
David Walker	
William Lloyd Garrison	
The Grimké Sisters	
Frederick Douglass	
Sojourner Truth	
Harriet Tubman	

B. Analyzing Causes and Recognizing Effects Use the chart below to record information about the relationship between abolition and women's rights.

Cause	Effect
Several abolitionists attended the World Anti-Slavery Convention in London in 1840. What happened to the women who attended?	**Elizabeth Cady Stanton and Lucretia Mott were angry about what happened.** What action did they take?

Guided Reading

A. Comparing and Contrasting As you read this section, use the chart below to take notes on the differences between the North and the South.

	North	South
Economy	1.	2.
Labor system	3.	4.
Views on slavery in the territories	5.	6.

B. Summarizing Use the chart below to take notes on the Compromise of 1850.

1. What role did these people play in passing the Compromise of 1850?
Henry Clay:
Daniel Webster:
Stephen A. Douglas:
2. What were the terms of the Compromise?

Chapter **15** *Section 2 The Crisis Deepens*

Guided Reading

A. Recognizing Effects As you read the section, take notes on the effects of the Compromise of 1850.

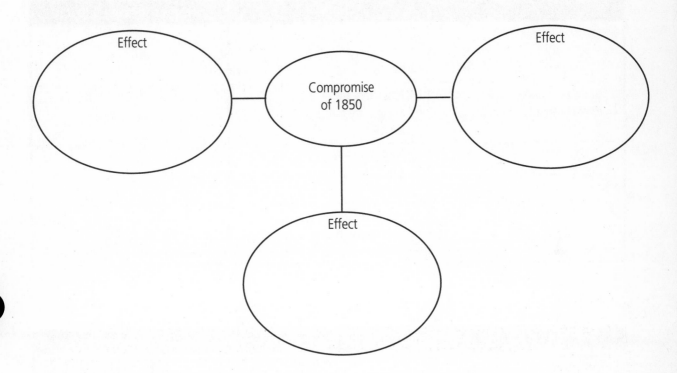

B. Evaluating Use the chart below to evaluate the role of these people and ideas in raising tensions over the issue of slavery in the 1850s.

popular sovereignty	1.
Kansas–Nebraska Act	2.
"Bleeding Kansas"	3.
John Brown	4.
Preston Brooks	5.

Guided Reading

A. Analyzing Points of View Use the chart below to take notes on people's views of the topics listed.

	Supporters	Reasons for their Support
1. *Dred Scott* decision	☐ Proslavery forces ☐ Antislavery forces ☐ Neither	
2. Douglas, in the Lincoln–Douglas debates	☐ Proslavery forces ☐ Antislavery forces ☐ Neither	
3. Lincoln, in the Lincoln–Douglas debates	☐ Proslavery forces ☐ Antislavery forces ☐ Neither	
4. John Brown's hanging	☐ Proslavery forces ☐ Antislavery forces ☐ Neither	

B. Finding Main Ideas Use the chart below to note something important you learned about each of the following.

Founding of the Republican Party:
John C. Frémont:
James Buchanan:

Guided Reading

A. Categorizing Use the chart below to take notes on the 1860 presidential election.

Party	Candidate	Platform	Supporters
1.			
2.			
3.			
4.			

B. Analyzing Points of View Use the chart below to take notes on the views of each group regarding secession.

Southerners	Northerners
1.	2.

Guided Reading

A. Summarizing As you read about the outbreak of the Civil War, summarize the
strengths and weaknesses of each side at the time war was declared.

1. What advantages did the Union have?

2. What advantages did the Confederacy have?

B. Summarizing As you read about the early days of the war, summarize the
Confederate strategy and the Union strategy.

1. What was the South's strategy?

2. What was the North's strategy?

C. Categorizing Fill in the chart below with information about two early battles of the
Civil War.

	Leaders	Outcome of the Battle	Important Facts
1. Fort Sumter			
2. First Battle of Bull Run			

D. Summarizing On the back of this paper, briefly explain the Anaconda Plan and King Cotton.

Guided Reading

A. Taking Notes As you read about the lives of ordinary soldiers, make notes about daily life in the military during the Civil War.

1. Who fought

2. How they were trained

3. What hardships they endured

4. How new technology affected soldiers

B. Summarizing On the back of this paper, briefly identify each of the following.

Monitor and *Merrimack*   rifle   minié ball

Guided Reading

A. Summarizing As you read about the ongoing Civil War, summarize the victories won by each side.

1. What victories did the Union win?

2. What victories did the Confederacy win?

B. Categorizing Fill in the chart below with information about two battles of the Civil War.

	Head of Union Forces	Head of Confederate Forces	Outcome of the Battle	Important Facts
1. Shiloh				
2. Antietam				

C. Finding Main Ideas On the back of this paper, briefly explain the Seven Days' Battles and who Ulysses S. Grant was.

Guided Reading

A. Analyzing Causes and Recognizing Effects As you read this section, use the boxes labeled *Causes* to explain why President Lincoln issued the Emancipation Proclamation. Use the boxes labeled *Effects* to record the results of the proclamation.

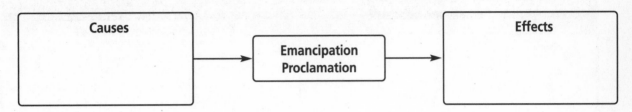

B. Identifying Opinions Use the chart below to record the different reactions to the Emancipation Proclamation.

EMANCIPATION PROCLAMATION	
Group	**Response**
Abolitionists	
Northern Democrats	
Union Soldiers	
White Southerners	
Black Southerners	

C. Solving Problems After the North began recruiting African-American soldiers into its army, Union officials wanted to pay black soldiers less than white soldiers. On the back of this paper, briefly explain the response of the 54th Massachusetts Regiment to this plan.

Guided Reading

A. Categorizing As you read this section, take notes about the different economic, social, and political changes that the Civil War brought about in the United States.

Civil War	
Economic Changes	**Social and Political Changes**

B. Summarizing As you read about Civil War prison camps, make a list of the conditions faced by prisoners in both the North and the South.

Conditions at Civil War Prison Camps

C. Analyzing Points of View On the back of this paper, briefly explain why many soldiers called the Civil War "a rich man's war but a poor man's fight."

Guided Reading

A. Sequencing Events As you read this section, record the major events of the Civil War between Antietam and the surrender at Appomattox.

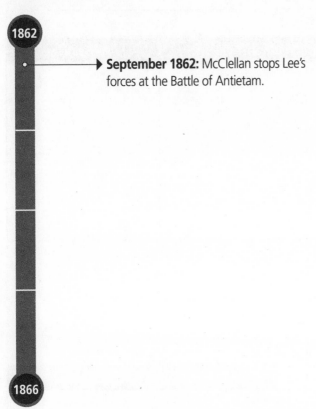

1862

September 1862: McClellan stops Lee's forces at the Battle of Antietam.

1866

B. Recognizing Effects Use the chart below to record the most important effects of the Union successes at Gettysburg and Vicksburg in July 1863.

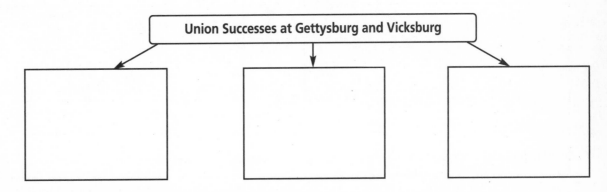

Union Successes at Gettysburg and Vicksburg

C. Making Inferences On the back of this paper, briefly explain how the following are related.

William Tecumseh Sherman   total war   1864 Reelection of Lincoln

Chapter **17** Section 4 The Legacy of the War

Guided Reading

A. Comparing and Contrasting As you read this section, compare and contrast the human costs of the Civil War in the North and the South.

	Northern Soldiers	Southern Soldiers	All Soldiers
Killed			
Wounded			

B. Finding Main Ideas In the boxes below, write a short paragraph explaining the significance of each event.

Passage of Thirteenth Amendment	Assassination of President Lincoln

C. Drawing Conclusions On the back of this paper, briefly explain the economic consequences of the Civil War in the South.

Guided Reading

A. Analyzing Points of View As you read pages 533–535, note how each person or group wanted to rebuild the South.

President Lincoln	
President Johnson	
Southern state governments	
Radical Republicans	

B. Finding Main Ideas As you read pages 535–536, note what was stated in these laws of the Reconstruction period.

Civil Rights Act of 1866	Fourteenth Amendment	Reconstruction Acts of 1867

C. Sequencing Events On the back of this paper, explain what led to President Johnson's impeachment trial and what its outcome was.

Name _____ Date _____

Guided Reading

A. Recognizing Effects As you read this section, answer the questions about changes for freed African Americans during Reconstruction.

1. Where did they go after slavery ended, and why?
2. How did they strengthen their families?
3. How were they educated?
4. Why did they want land, and why didn't they get it?
5. What was it like for them to work under the contract system?
6. What was it like for them to work under the sharecropping system?
7. How did the Ku Klux Klan affect their lives?

B. Making Inferences On the back of this paper, tell what you think would have happened if freed people had been guaranteed their own plots of land.

Chapter **18** *Section 3 End of Reconstruction*

Guided Reading

A. Analyzing Causes and Recognizing Effects As you read this section, note how each event strengthened or weakened Reconstruction.

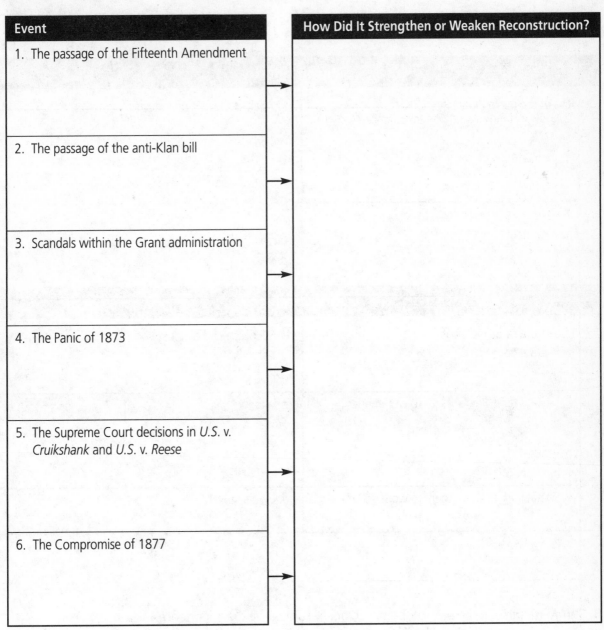

Event	How Did It Strengthen or Weaken Reconstruction?
1. The passage of the Fifteenth Amendment	
2. The passage of the anti-Klan bill	
3. Scandals within the Grant administration	
4. The Panic of 1873	
5. The Supreme Court decisions in *U.S.* v. *Cruikshank* and *U.S.* v. *Reese*	
6. The Compromise of 1877	

B. Summarizing On the back of this paper, summarize the successes and failures of Reconstruction for African Americans.

Guided Reading

A. Taking Notes As you read this section, take notes on the rise and fall of the mining and cattle industries in the West.

Mining Industry	
1. Rise of the mining industry	2. Fall of the mining industry

Cattle Industry	
3. Rise of the cattle industry	4. Fall of the cattle industry

B. Summarizing On the back of this paper, briefly summarize the importance of each of the following in the settlement of the West.

boomtown   *vaquero*   vigilante

Guided Reading

A. Sequencing Events As you read about the conflicts that occurred during the settlement of the Western frontier, answer questions about the time line below.

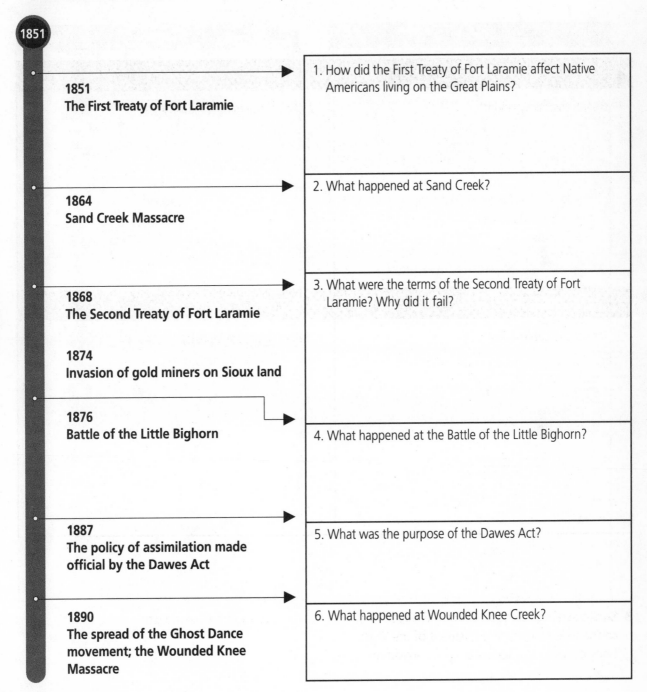

1851

1851
The First Treaty of Fort Laramie

1. How did the First Treaty of Fort Laramie affect Native Americans living on the Great Plains?

1864
Sand Creek Massacre

2. What happened at Sand Creek?

1868
The Second Treaty of Fort Laramie

3. What were the terms of the Second Treaty of Fort Laramie? Why did it fail?

1874
Invasion of gold miners on Sioux land

1876
Battle of the Little Bighorn

4. What happened at the Battle of the Little Bighorn?

1887
The policy of assimilation made official by the Dawes Act

5. What was the purpose of the Dawes Act?

1890
The spread of the Ghost Dance movement; the Wounded Knee Massacre

6. What happened at Wounded Knee Creek?

B. Summarizing On the back of this paper, briefly summarize why the Dawes Act failed.

Guided Reading

A. Analyzing Causes and Recognizing Effects As you read about life in the West in this section, supply the missing causes or effects.

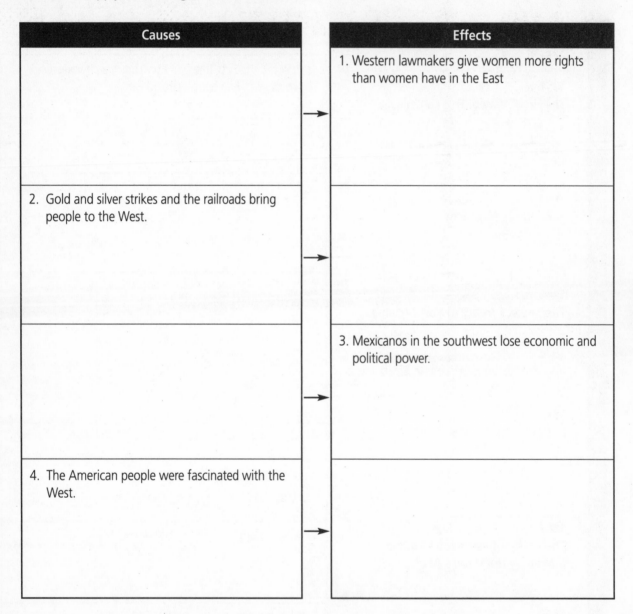

Causes	Effects
	1. Western lawmakers give women more rights than women have in the East
2. Gold and silver strikes and the railroads bring people to the West.	
	3. Mexicanos in the southwest lose economic and political power.
4. The American people were fascinated with the West.	

B. Forming and Supporting Opinions On the back of this page, briefly explain why you think that the American people were so fascinated by the myth of the Old West.

Guided Reading

A. Drawing Conclusions As you read this section, take notes to answer questions about the conditions that made farming increasingly unprofitable.

In the late 1800s, farmers faced rising costs and falling crop prices.

1. Why had farming become unprofitable?	
2. Why did farmers support "free silver"?	

Farmers and farm organizations, such as the Grange, found support in the federal government and in populism and the Populist Party.

3. How did the federal government aid the farmers?	
4. What reforms did the Populist Party call for?	

In the 1896 election, William Jennings Bryan, the candidate supported by the Populist Party, lost to Republican candidate William McKinley.

5. What economic plan did Bryan support, and who voted for him?	
6. What economic plan did McKinley support, and who voted for him?	

B. Analyzing Points of View On the back of this paper, briefly explain Frederick Jackson Turner's theory about the frontier.

Guided Reading

A. Analyzing Causes After the Civil War, the United States was still a mostly rural nation. By the 1920s, it had become the leading industrial nation of the world. This immense change was caused by several factors. Answer the questions for two of the factors.

→ **Factor 1: Abundant Natural Resources**

1. Which resources played crucial roles in industrialization?	2. How did Edwin L. Drake help industry to acquire larger quantities of oil?	3. How did the Bessemer process increase steel production?	4. What new uses for steel were developed at this time?

→ **Factor 2: Increasing Number of Inventions**

5. How did Thomas Edison contribute to this development?	6. How did Alexander Graham Bell contribute?	7. How did Isaac Singer contribute?	8. How did Christopher Latham Sholes contribute?

B. Finding Main Ideas On the back of this page, explain the importance of the following terms.

patent   business cycle   generator

Guided Reading

A. Comparing As you read, take notes about the two companies that built the transcontinental railroad.

Central Pacific	Union Pacific
_____	_____
_____	_____
_____	_____
_____	_____

B. Recognizing Effects Take notes to answer these questions about the impact of the railroads.

1. How did the railroads affect time?	2. How did the railroads affect the economy?
3. How did the railroads change the population of the West?	4. In what way did the railroads give people control of the environment?

Chapter **20** Section 3 The Rise of Big Business

Guided Reading

A. Analyzing Causes As you read this section, answer the questions below about factors that led to the growth of big business.

   a. What is it?

   b. How did it help businesses to grow?

1. Corporation	a. b.
2. Monopoly	a. b.
3. Trust	a. b.

B. Comparing and Contrasting Use the chart to compare and contrast John D. Rockefeller and Andrew Carnegie.

	Rockefeller	Carnegie
1. Did he start life poor or rich?		
2. What industry did he control?		
3. What methods did he use to gain control?		
4. How did he try to do good for others?		

Guided Reading

A. Finding Main Ideas As you read about labor and management, answer the questions below.

1. What conditions led to the formation of labor unions?

Union	What did this union do?
2. Knights of Labor	
3. American Railway Union	
4. American Federation of Labor	

Strikes and Violence	What happened?
5. Railroad Strike, 1877	
6. Haymarker affair, 1886	
7. Homestead Strike, 1892	
8. Pullman Strike, 1894	

B. Analyzing Causes On the back of this paper, identify who Mary Harris "Mother" Jones was and why workers loved her.

Chapter **21** Section 1 Cities Grow and Change

Guided Reading

A. Recognizing Effects As you read this section, use the chart below to take notes on the effects of industrialization on American cities.

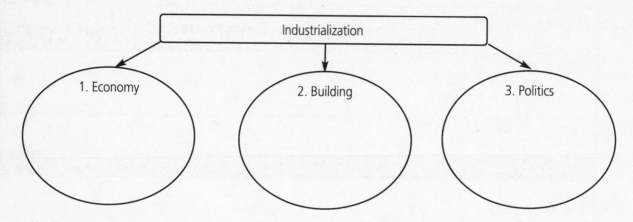

B. Identifying and Solving Problems Use the chart below to take notes on how people addressed important issues in U.S. cities around 1900.

Problems / Issues	Solution
4. Overcrowding	
5. Poverty	
6. Immigration	

Chapter **21** *Section 2 The New Immigrants*

Guided Reading

A. Comparing and Contrasting As you read the section, use the chart below to take notes on the experiences of the new immigrants.

	Immigrant Experiences
Points of Entry	
Finding a Home and a Job	
Assimilating into American Culture	
Facing Discrimination	

B. Finding Main Ideas Use the back of this page to define the following concepts.

new immigrants   melting pot

Chapter 21 *Section 3 Segregation and Discrimination*

Guided Reading

A. Finding Main Ideas Use the chart below to take notes on how the topics listed affected racial equality around 1900.

	What was it?	Who did it affect?
1. Literacy test		
2. Poll tax		
3. Grandfather clause		
4. Jim Crow laws		
5. Segregation		
6. *Plessy* v. *Ferguson*		
7. NAACP		

B. Evaluating On the back of this page, evaluate the role that the following people played in opposing discrimination.

Booker T. Washington   W. E. B. Du Bois   Ida B. Wells

Guided Reading

A. Recognizing Effects Use the chart below to take notes on how each of the following contributed to the emergence of mass culture in the United States around 1900.

New Activity	Effect
Increased education	1.
Advertising	2.
World's Fairs	3.
Sports	4.
Movies	5.

B. Evaluating On the back of this page, explain how each of the following people or items contributed to the growth of mass culture.

Joseph Pulitzer   William Randolph Hearst   department stores

mail-order catalogs   vaudeville   ragtime

Name _____ Date _____

Guided Reading Workbook: Unit 7

Chapter **22** *Section 1 Roosevelt and Progressivism*

Guided Reading

A. Categorizing As you read about the era of reform, list several examples of each of the three basic goals of Progressivism.

1. Reforming government and expanding democracy

2. Promoting social welfare

3. Creating economic reform

B. Taking Notes As you read this section, write notes to answer questions about President Theodore Roosevelt. If Roosevelt took no steps to solve the problem or if no legislation was involved in solving the problem, write "none."

Problem	What steps did Roosevelt take to solve each problem?	Which legislation helped solve the problem?
1. Trusts		
2. Dangerous foods and medicines		
3. Shrinking wilderness and natural resources		

C. Summarizing On the back of this paper, explain the importance of each of the following.

muckrakers   Sherman Antitrust Act   Theodore Roosevelt

Chapter 22 Section 2 Taft and Wilson as Progressives

Guided Reading

A. Taking Notes As you read about Taft's and Wilson's approach to reform, take notes to answer the questions.

What were the aims of each piece of legislation or constitutional amendment?
1. Sixteenth Amendment
2. Seventeenth Amendment
3. Clayton Antitrust Act
4. Federal Reserve Act
5. Eighteenth Amendment

B. Summarizing On the back of this paper, explain the importance of William Howard Taft as a progressive, a president, a Republican, and a chief justice.

Chapter **22** *Section 3 Women Win New Rights*

Guided Reading

A. Taking Notes As you read this section, take notes about each of the following women.

1. Lillian Wald
2. Jane Addams
3. Charlotte Perkins Gilman
4. Carry Nation
5. Susan B. Anthony
6. Carrie Chapman Catt

B. Summarizing On the back of this paper, explain the significance of the Nineteenth Amendment.

Guided Reading

A. Analyzing Causes As you read this section, use the chart below to explain the main reasons for the emergence of the United States as an imperial power.

The Roots of American Imperialism		
1. Economic interests	2. Military interests	3. Belief in cultural superiority

B. Finding Main Ideas Use the chart below to describe the role played by each person or group in the history of U.S. involvement in Hawaii.

U.S. Imperialism in Hawaii	
Christian missionaries	
American planters	
Queen Liliuokalani	
U.S. Marines	
Benjamin Harrison	
Grover Cleveland	

C. Summarizing On the back of this paper, explain how the United States acquired Alaska.

Guided Reading

A. Sequencing Events As you read this section, use the time line below to record significant events of the Spanish-American War.

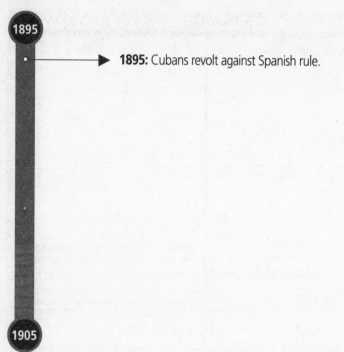

1895: Cubans revolt against Spanish rule.

B. Analyzing Effects Use the chart below to record important results of the Spanish–American War.

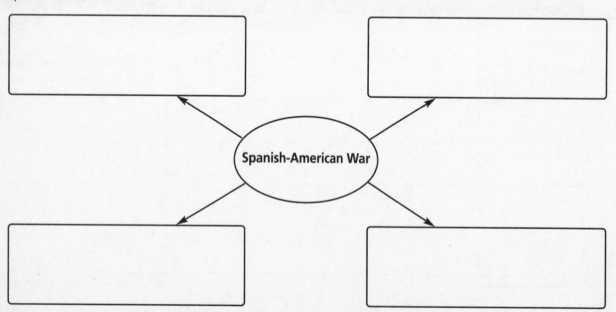

Spanish-American War

C. Analyzing Points of View On the back of this paper, explain why members of the Anti-Imperialist League became disappointed in U.S. foreign policy at the turn of the century.

Name _____ Date _____

Guided Reading

A. Finding Main Ideas Use the chart below to record information about U.S. involvement in China.

The United States in China		
Spheres of Influence	Open Door Policy	Boxer Rebellion

B. Analyzing Causes and Recognizing Effects Use the chart below to explain the reasons for the United States interest in building a canal and the effects of the canal's construction.

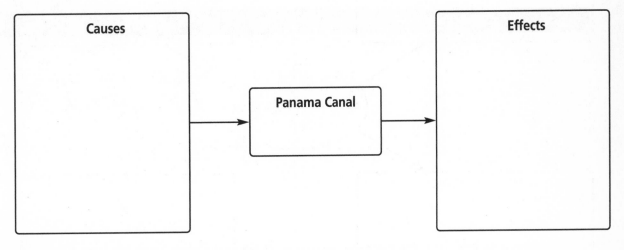

Causes

Panama Canal

Effects

C. Summarizing On the back of this paper, explain how Theodore Roosevelt changed the Monroe Doctrine.

Guided Reading

A. Analyzing Causes As you read pages 679–680, note on the chart how each of the following causes led to World War I.

1. Imperialism	2. Nationalism	3. Militarism	4. Alliances	5. Archduke's Assassination

B. Contrasting As you read pages 680–681, fill in the chart. Describe the new style of warfare and the new weapons that made World War I different from earlier wars.

Trench Warfare	New Weapons

C. Sequencing Events On the back of this page, make a time line showing four events that led the United States to declare war on Germany. Start with May 1915.

Chapter **24** *Section 2 America Joins the Fight*

Guided Reading

A. Finding Main Ideas As you read this section, answer the following questions about the American experience in World War I.

1. How did the United States raise an army and navy?
2. How did women and African-American men serve in the war?
3. How did U.S. naval officers help the Allies?
4. How did U.S. ground troops help the Allies?
5. Who were some American heroes of the war?
6. What ended the war?
7. What were the human costs of the war?

B. Analyzing Points of View If you had been an African-American soldier, how might you have felt about serving overseas during the war? Answer on the back of this paper.

Chapter **24** *Section 3 Life on the Home Front*

Guided Reading

A. Recognizing Effects As you read pages 691–693, answer the questions about life for American civilians during World War I.

1. How did the U.S. government raise money to fight the war?	2. How did the government get enough food and supplies to send to Europe?
3. How did the government get people to support the war?	4. How did the government react to antiwar activities?

B. Comparing As you read pages 693–694, fill in the chart. Note the war's economic effects on African Americans, Mexicans, and women. Below the chart, briefly state what was similar about their experiences.

African Americans	Mexicans	Women

C. Forming and Supporting Opinions On the back of this paper, write whether you agree or disagree with the Supreme Court's decision in *Schenck* v. *United States*. Give reasons for your opinion.

Chapter 24 *Section 4 The Legacy of World War I*

Guided Reading

A. Finding Main Ideas As you read about the war's outcome on pages 695–696, note what President Wilson proposed in his Fourteen Points and what European nations demanded in the Treaty of Versailles.

1. Fourteen Points	2. Treaty of Versailles

3. What did the two peace plans have in common?

B. Analyzing Causes Postwar crises made Americans want a "return to normalcy." As you read pages 697–698, briefly note how each set of events harmed the country.

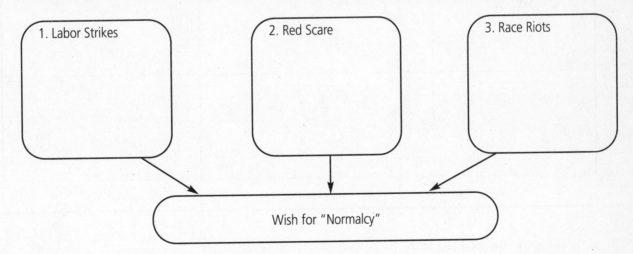

1. Labor Strikes

2. Red Scare

3. Race Riots

Wish for "Normalcy"

C. Making Decisions If you had been a U.S. senator in 1919, would you have voted for or against the Treaty of Versailles and the League of Nations? Explain your decision on the back of this paper.

Chapter **25** Section 1 The Business of America

Guided Reading

A. Recognizing Effects As you read this section, fill in the second column with a description of the effect on American life of the inventions and trends listed in column one.

Invention or Trend	Effects of the Invention or Trend
1. automobiles	
2. airplanes	
3. cheap fuel	
4. modern advertising	
5. installment buying	

B. Summarizing On the back of this paper, briefly summarize the business policies of Presidents Warren G. Harding and Calvin Coolidge.

Chapter **25** Section 2 Changes in Society

Guided Reading

A. Finding Main Ideas As you read this section, fill in the diagram below with the main ideas about the changes in American society in the Roaring Twenties.

Youth in the Twenties	New Roles for Women

Changes in American Society

Changes for African Americans	A Divided Society

B. Drawing Conclusions On the back of this paper, answer the question "How did Prohibition change society?"

Name _____   Date _____

Guided Reading

A. Categorizing As you read this section about how America's popular culture developed in the 1920s, give examples in each area of popular culture.

1. Movies	2. Books and magazines
3. Radio	4. Sports
5. Music	6. Literature

B. Summarizing On the back of this paper, briefly explain the importance of each of the following in the development of American popular culture of the 1920s.

mass media   Harlem Renaissance   Lost Generation

Guided Reading

A. Analyzing Causes As you read this section, take notes to describe the problems that existed in the economy at the end of the 1920s.

	Problems in the Economy
Agriculture	
Income distribution	
Industry	
Consumer debt	
Stock market	

B. Finding Main Ideas Answer the questions below about President Hoover's actions during the early years of the Great Depression.

President Hoover's Actions
1. Why didn't Hoover want the federal government to interfere in the economy?
2. What did Hoover propose as solutions for the Depression?
3. How did Hoover respond to the Bonus Army?

C. Recognizing Effects On the back of this page, explain how most Americans responded to Hoover's policies and actions.

Guided Reading

A. Solving Problems As you read this section, use the chart below to take notes about the first steps President Roosevelt took to fight the Great Depression.

Bank Holiday	Fireside Chats	New Deal

B. Analyzing Points of View Use the chart below to record various responses to the New Deal.

	Response to the New Deal
conservatives	
Huey Long	
Father Charles Coughlin	
Francis Townshend	

C. Finding Main Ideas Use the back of this page to explain the importance of each of these terms.

Social Security Act   Second New Deal   "court-packing" bill   deficit spending

Guided Reading

A. Recognizing Effects As you read this section, use the chart below to summarize the experiences of the following groups during the Depression.

1. Farmers in the Dust Bowl
2. Families
3. Writers and photographers
4. Women
5. Minorities
6. Unions

B. Finding Main Ideas Use the back of this page to explain the importance of each of these terms and names.

Dust Bowl   Eleanor Roosevelt   Congress of Industrial Organizations (CIO)   sit-down strike

Name _____ Date _____

Guided Reading

A. Recognizing Effects As you read this section, use the chart below to record how the Great Depression and the New Deal changed individuals and the federal government.

Changes to Individuals	Changes to Federal Government

B. Finding Main Ideas In the chart below, record the answers to the following questions about the legacy of the New Deal today.

1. What New Deal program continues to provide old-age pensions, and how do people view it today?	
2. If a bank closes today, what does the FDIC do for depositors?	
3. How does the Securities and Exchange Commission try to prevent another stock market crash?	
4. What is the difference between a conservative and a liberal?	

Guided Reading

A. Comparing and Contrasting Use the chart below to take notes on the dictators that came to power in Europe during the 1920s and 1930s.

Dictator	When and where he came to power	Political philosophy
Benito Mussolini	1.	2.
Adolf Hitler	3.	4.
Joseph Stalin	5.	6.

B. Sequencing Events Use the time line below to take notes on the events that led to the start of World War II and U.S. participation in the war.

1936

1936 Germany and Italy form Axis. Civil war erupts in Spain.

1. What role did Germany and Italy play in the Spanish Civil War?

1938 Germany annexes Austria.

Britain and France allow Germany to annex the Sudetenland in the Munich Agreement.

2. Why did Britain and France agree to let Germany annex the Sudetenland?

1939 Germany invades Czechoslovakia.

Germany signs nonaggression pact with the Soviet Union.

Germany invades Poland.

Britain and France declare war on Germany.

3. Why did the Soviet Union sign the nonaggression pact with Germany?

1940 Japan joins Axis. Germany invades France. Battle of Britain fought.

4. Why did Japan attack the United States?

1941 Germany invades the Soviet Union.

1941 Japan attacks United States at Pearl Harbor.

1942

Guided Reading

A. Sequencing Events Use the time line below to take notes on the course of the war in Africa and Europe.

1941

1941	Dec.	The United States enters the war.
1942	June	British stop Axis advance in Africa at the Battle of El Alamein.
	Sept.	Germans attack Soviet city of Stalingrad.
	Nov.	American forces join the Allies in North Africa.
1943	Feb.	Soviets win the Battle of Stalingrad.
	May	Axis in North Africa surrender to Allies.
	July	Allies invade Sicily.
	Sept.	Italy surrenders to the Allies.
1944	June	Allies invade France at Normandy.
	Dec.	Battle of the Bulge fought.
1945	May	Soviet army captures Berlin and Germany surrenders.

1946

1. Why did the Allies drive the Axis out of Africa before invading France?

2. What was the significance of the Battle of Stalingrad?

3. Why were the Germans surprised by the Allied invasion at Normandy?

4. What was the significance of the Battle of the Bulge?

B. Finding Main Ideas Use the back of this page to write a brief paragraph explaining the significance of the following terms.

Yalta Conference   Holocaust

Guided Reading

A. Sequencing Events Use the time line below to take notes on the course of the war in the Pacific.

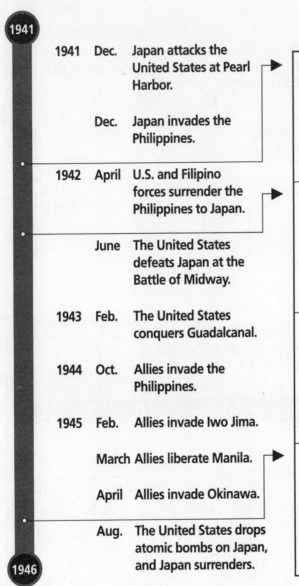

1941

1941	Dec.	Japan attacks the United States at Pearl Harbor.
	Dec.	Japan invades the Philippines.
1942	April	U.S. and Filipino forces surrender the Philippines to Japan.
	June	The United States defeats Japan at the Battle of Midway.
1943	Feb.	The United States conquers Guadalcanal.
1944	Oct.	Allies invade the Philippines.
1945	Feb.	Allies invade Iwo Jima.
	March	Allies liberate Manila.
	April	Allies invade Okinawa.
	Aug.	The United States drops atomic bombs on Japan, and Japan surrenders.

1946

1. What happened to the American and Filipino troops that surrendered on the Philippines?

2. What was the significance of the Battle of Midway?

3. What were three Pacific islands that the United States invaded in the war against Japan?

4. How many people were killed by the atomic bomb dropped on Hiroshima?

B. Finding Main Ideas Use the back of this page to write a brief paragraph explaining the significance of the following terms.

island hopping   Manhattan Project

Chapter **27** Section 4 The Home Front

Guided Reading

A. Finding Main Ideas Use the chart below to take notes on how each of the following factors contributed to the wartime economy.

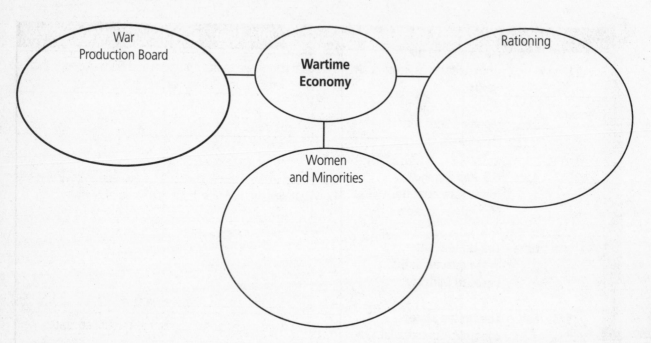

B. Recognizing Effects Use the chart below to take notes on how the war affected the following groups.

Group	Effects of the War
Women	
African Americans	
Mexican Americans	
Japanese Americans	

Guided Reading

A. Recognizing Effects Use the chart below to take notes on the casualties suffered by the following nations from 1939 to 1945.

Nation	Dead	Wounded	Total
Soviet Union	1.		
Germany	2.		
China	3.		
Japan	4.		
United States	5.		
Great Britain	6.		
France	7.		
Italy	8.		

B. Finding Main Ideas Use the chart below to write a brief paragraph explaining the significance of the following items.

1. Marshall Plan	2. G.I. Bill of Rights
3. Nuremberg trials	4. United Nations

Guided Reading

A. Identifying and Solving Problems As you read this section, describe the solutions offered to deal with postwar problems.

> **1. Problem: Severe housing shortage**
>
> Solution offered by developers such as William Levitt:

> **2. Problem: Labor strikes that threaten to cripple the nation**
>
> Solution offered by the Truman administration:

> **3. Problem: Discrimination and racial violence**
>
> Solution offered during the Truman administration:

B. Recognizing Effects As you read this section, complete the cause-and-effect diagram with the specific U.S. actions made in response to the Soviet actions listed. Use the following terms and names in filling out the diagram:

containment   Truman Doctrine   Berlin airlift

Cause: Soviet Action	**Effect: U.S. Action**
Soviet leader Joseph Stalin refused free elections in Eastern Europe and set up pro-Soviet governments.	1.

Cause: Soviet Action	**Effect: U.S. Action**
Soviets blockaded Berlin for almost a year.	2.

C. Summarizing On the back of this paper, explain the significance of each of the following terms.

Fair Deal   Cold War   Marshall Plan

Guided Reading

A. Finding Main Ideas As you read this section, fill out the chart below by writing answers to the questions in the appropriate boxes.

	Civil War in China	Civil War in Korea
1. Which side did the United States support, and why?		
2. What was the outcome of the war?		

B. Recognizing Effects As you read this section, write your answers to the question in the appropriate boxes.

	How did the United States react, and why?
1. In 1956, Britain, France, and Israel invaded Egypt and occupied the Suez Canal.	
2. In 1957, the Soviet Union launched Sputnik.	
3. In 1960, the Soviet Union brought down an American U-2 piloted by Francis Gary Powers.	

C. Summarizing On the back of this paper, explain the significance of each of the following terms and names.

brinksmanship   38th parallel   Joseph McCarthy

Guided Reading

A. Recognizing Effects As you read this section, write notes about how Americans were affected by various trends of the 1950s.

Trends	Effects
1. Suburban expansion: flight from the cities	
2. Baby boom	
3. Dramatic increase in the use of the automobile	
4. The rise of consumerism	

B. Taking Notes As you read this section, take notes to answer questions about innovations and trends in 1950s popular culture.

1. Television	What are some of the most popular shows?
2. Rock 'n' roll	Who helped to popularize it?

C. Summarizing On the back of this paper, explain the significance of the following terms.

suburb   sunbelt   rock 'n' roll

Guided Reading

A. Analyzing Causes As you read this section, use the chart below to explain why the African-American struggle for equal rights became more successful following World War II.

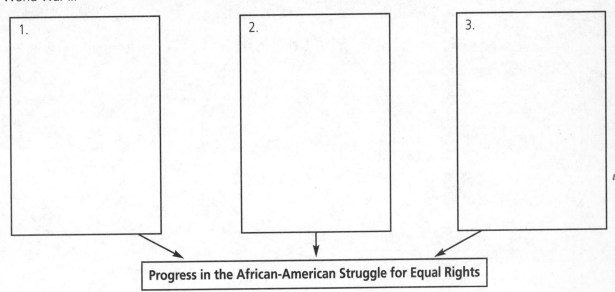

| 1. | 2. | 3. |

Progress in the African-American Struggle for Equal Rights

B. Finding Main Ideas African Americans won important battles of the civil rights movement in the courts. However, without the struggle of many others in their own communities, the movement would have been less successful. Use the chart below to describe some of these important victories.

	Civil Rights Victories
Montgomery, Alabama	
Little Rock, Arkansas	
Greensboro, North Carolina	

C. Recognizing Effects On the back of this paper, describe the short- and long-term effects of the Supreme Court's decision in *Brown* v. *Board of Education of Topeka.*

Guided Reading

A. Comparing and Contrasting As you read this section, compare and contrast the work of Presidents Kennedy and Johnson on civil rights issues.

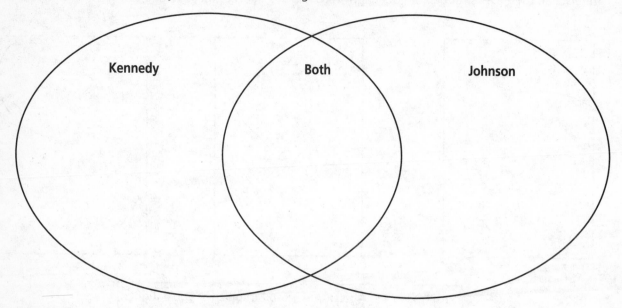

Kennedy   Both   Johnson

B. Finding Main Ideas During his presidency, Lyndon Johnson became a great supporter of social reforms. Johnson's reform program became known as the Great Society. Use the chart below to describe important legislation passed during the Johnson administration.

	Johnson's Great Society
Civil Rights Act (1964)	
Voting Rights Act (1965)	
Medical Care Act (1965)	
Elementary and Secondary School Act (1965)	

C. Making Inferences During the civil rights era, violent reactions to the African-American struggle for equality were often broadcast on television. Use the back of this paper to explain what effect these broadcasts may have had on the movement.

Name _____   Date _____

Guided Reading

A. Making Generalizations Use the chart below to briefly describe how the African-American struggle for equal rights inspired other groups to fight for their civil rights.

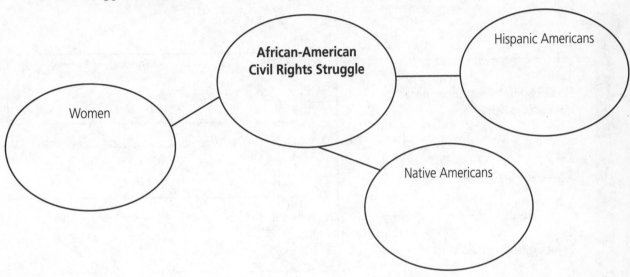

B. Comparing and Contrasting Many Hispanic Americans were inspired by the African-American civil rights struggle. Use the chart below to explain what characteristics of the Hispanic community may have helped them unite in their struggle for equal rights. Also list factors that might have hindered their struggle.

Hispanic American Civil Rights Movement	
Factors promoting unity	Factors hindering unity

C. Summarizing On the back of this paper, write a brief history of the Equal Rights Amendment.

Guided Reading

A. Sequencing Events As you read this section, take notes to answer questions about the roots of the conflict in Vietnam.

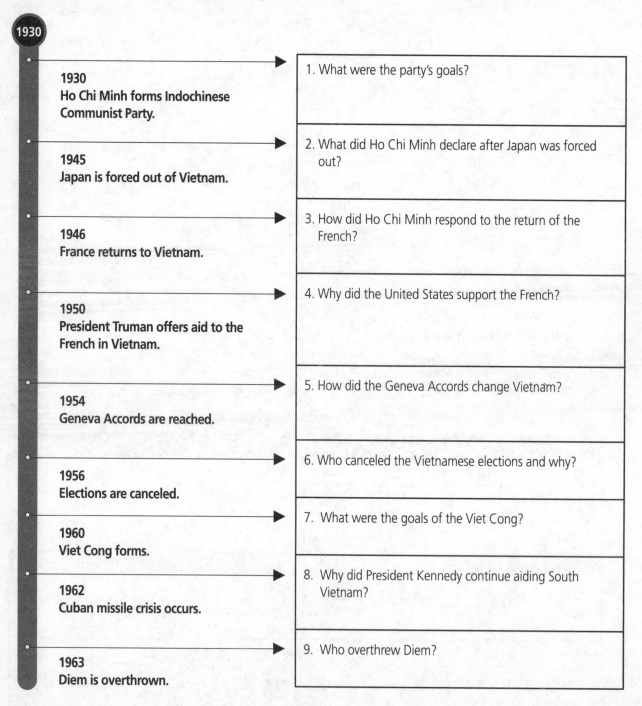

1930

1930
Ho Chi Minh forms Indochinese Communist Party.

1. What were the party's goals?

1945
Japan is forced out of Vietnam.

2. What did Ho Chi Minh declare after Japan was forced out?

1946
France returns to Vietnam.

3. How did Ho Chi Minh respond to the return of the French?

1950
President Truman offers aid to the French in Vietnam.

4. Why did the United States support the French?

1954
Geneva Accords are reached.

5. How did the Geneva Accords change Vietnam?

1956
Elections are canceled.

6. Who canceled the Vietnamese elections and why?

1960
Viet Cong forms.

7. What were the goals of the Viet Cong?

1962
Cuban missile crisis occurs.

8. Why did President Kennedy continue aiding South Vietnam?

1963
Diem is overthrown.

9. Who overthrew Diem?

B. Finding Main Ideas On the back of this paper, summarize the domino theory and explain how it led to U.S. involvement in Vietnam.

Guided Reading

A. Analyzing Causes As you read pages 841–842, fill in the diagram with reasons why the war frustrated U.S. soldiers.

Frustrations for U.S. Soldiers

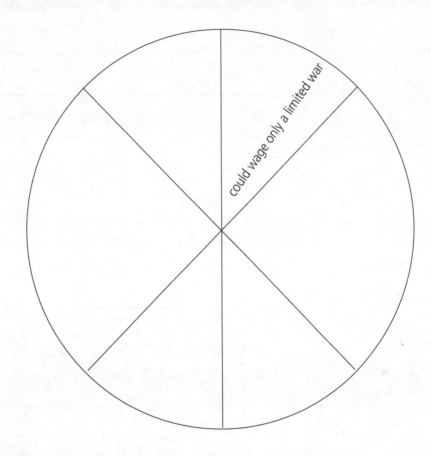

could wage only a limited war

B. Recognizing Effects As you read pages 842–845, note how each war tactic on the chart affected Vietnamese and American soldiers or civilians.

War Tactic	Effects on Vietnamese	Effects on Americans
1. Napalm		
2. Agent Orange		
3. Search-and-destroy missions		
4. Tet offensive		
5. My Lai massacre		

Guided Reading

A. Analyzing Points of View As you read pages 846–848, note the reasons that Americans opposed the war in Vietnam.

Reasons for Opposing the War

B. Recognizing Effects As you read pages 848-849, write down effects of the war, both in Asia and the United States.

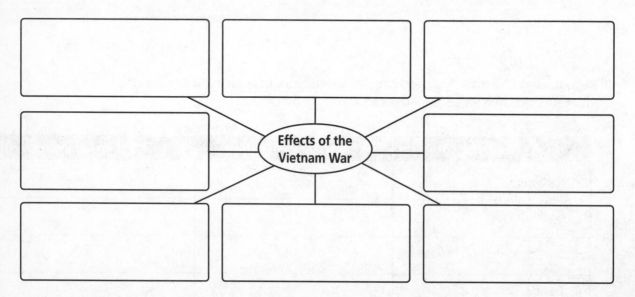

Effects of the Vietnam War

C. Drawing Conclusions On the back of this paper, write what you think would have happened if President Nixon had not withdrawn U.S. troops from Vietnam in 1973. Give reasons for your conclusions.

Guided Reading

A. Solving Problems As you read this section, fill in the second column of the chart below with the details of how President Nixon attempted to solve the problems that he faced in office.

Problems	Nixon's Solutions
1. Size and power of the Federal government	
2. Civil unrest	
3. Economic crisis	
4. U.S.-China relations	
5. U.S.-Soviet relations	

B. Summarizing On the back of this page, briefly explain the importance of each of the following during the Nixon years.

revenue sharing　　　Henry Kissinger　　　détente

Chapter **31** *Section 2 Watergate Brings Down Nixon*

Guided Reading

A. Sequencing Events As you read this section about Watergate, answer the questions about the time line.

1972

1972
June Break-in at Democratic
       Campaign office

Nov. Nixon wins reelection

| 1. How were the burglars connected to President Nixon? |

1973
Feb. Senate begins Watergate
       investigation

Mar. Nixon okays "hush money" to
       Watergate burglars

| 2. What did the following men tell the Senate about Nixon: |
| a. John Dean? |
| |
| b. a White House aide? |

Oct. Vice-President Spiro Agnew
       resigns

1974
Jan. House Judiciary Committee
       opens impeachment hearings

| 3. Why was Agnew forced to resign? |

July Judiciary Committee votes on
       impeachment

Aug. Unedited tapes are released

| 4. What was the Judiciary committee vote on impeachment? |

President Nixon resigns

| 5. What happened after Nixon resigned? |

B. Recognizing Effects On the other side of this paper, briefly explain the effects of the Watergate scandal on the nation.

Guided Reading

A. Taking Notes As you read about Presidents Ford and Carter, take notes to describe the policies of each toward the problems facing them.

Problems Faced by Ford	Policies
1. Ending Watergate scandal	
2. Troubled economy	
3. Relations with Congress	
4. Southeast Asia	
5. Cold War tensions	

Problems Faced by Carter	Policies
1. Distrust of politicians	
2. Relations with Congress	
3. Energy crisis	
4. Troubled economy	
5. Panama Canal	
6. Middle East tensions	
7. Environment	
8. Iran hostage crisis	

B. Making Inferences On the back of this paper, explain the importance of the pardon of Nixon to the presidency of Gerald Ford and the failure to win quick release of the hostages to the presidency of Jimmy Carter.

Name _____   Date _____

Guided Reading

A. Summarizing Take notes about the important events of the Reagan, Bush, and Clinton presidencies by answering the following questions.

The Reagan Presidency
1. What were President Reagan's conservative goals?
2. What was the Iran-Contra affair?

The Bush Presidency
3. What took place in foreign affairs during President Bush's term?

The Clinton Presidency
4. What laws or programs did President Clinton succeed in passing?
5. Why was Clinton impeached, and what happened at the Senate trial?

B. Finding Main Ideas On the back of this page, explain the following terms.

supply-side economics   Persian Gulf War   NAFTA

Guided Reading

A. Analyzing Causes and Recognizing Effects As you read about changes to technology and the economy, complete the chart by filling in the cause or effect.

Causes	Effects
1.	By 1996, about 71 percent of American workers had jobs in the service industry.
2. Technology changed the way information was delivered and gave people access to more information.	
3.	Factory workers lost jobs.
4. Many corporations engaged in downsizing.	
5. Because of global trade, the economies of various countries became more closely linked.	
6. Scientists developed new drugs.	

B. Finding Main Ideas On the back of this paper, define the following terms.

    e-commerce   service economy   information revolution

Guided Reading

A. Recognizing Effects As you read this section, answer the following questions about the way immigration is changing the United States.

1. From what two areas of the world did most recent immigrants come?	
2. How are these immigrants changing the makeup of U.S. society?	

B. Analyzing Points of View Use the chart below to take notes about the different views about immigration.

1. Why do some people think immigration hurts the economy?	2. Why do some people think immigration helps the economy?

C. Finding Main Ideas On the back of this page, identify the following term.
Immigration Reform and Control Act of 1981

ISBN 0-618-15628-3

90000>

9 780618 156283

2-01340

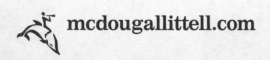

mcdougallittell.com